Arena Mina

Elisabeth P. Redon

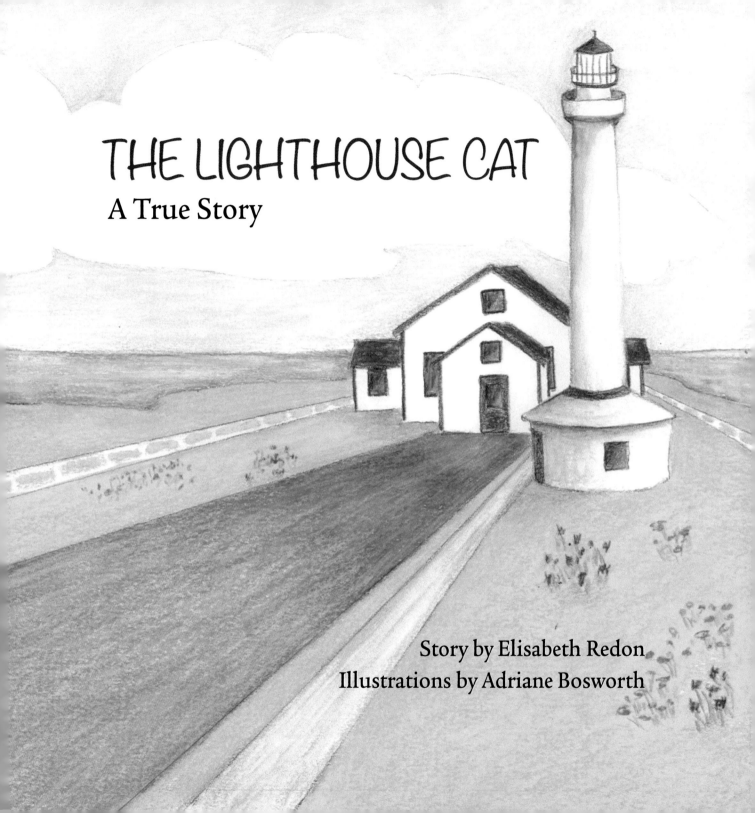

THE LIGHTHOUSE CAT

A True Story

Story by Elisabeth Redon
Illustrations by Adriane Bosworth

It began in late summer when visitors came
To see a lighthouse with the Point Arena name.

At this lighthouse someone left an unwanted cat.
Feeling hungry and terrified, for hours she sat.

This adorable, little, affectionate cat
Was abandoned at the water tank, just like that.

Beyond the water tank a lighthouse was in sight.
She hoped to find shelter as she raced toward the light.

Running past the houses where visitors slept,
She hid in a culvert where many creatures met.

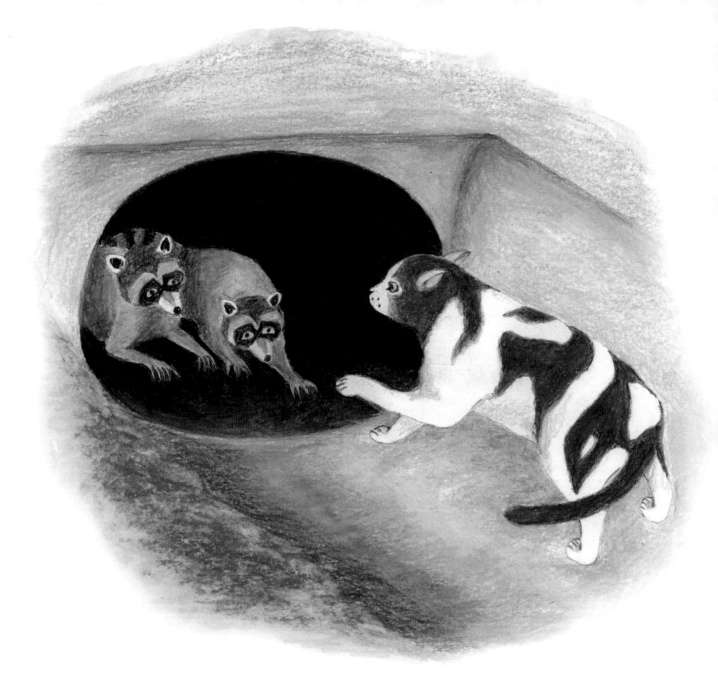

In this culvert she found twin raccoons staying there.
It was THEIR hiding place, but they agreed to share.

She slept a long time, no food or water for her.
How could she live like this with no reason to purr?

Hungry and thirsty for days, she finally found
Fresh food and water carefully placed on the ground.

She wondered who would leave food and water for her.
It must be someone who wanted to hear her purr.

It was then she saw a kind-looking man named Mark.
She made sure he would see her even in the dark.

Mark, the Lighthouse Director, saw this hungry cat,
And gradually coaxed her to come where he sat.

When she began to explain her very sad tale,
She found that he listened as he opened the mail.

She meowed and meowed while sitting in Mark's lap,
Telling her story as she curled up for a nap.

Now she feels loved and cared for and very well fed,
But when the lighthouse gate closes, where is her bed?

By late afternoon, when all the lighthouse tours end,
She is carried to a shelter by her new friend.

She sleeps for the night unless disturbed by a mouse
In this nice shelter, which is her new little house.

Now that she has a wonderful, new home at last,
This happy lighthouse cat needs a new name, and fast.

Many visitors made up names for this cute cat,
The name, "Arena Mina," was perfect for that.

Arena Mina, the Lighthouse Cat, loves her home.
Come visit soon and watch for Mina while you roam.

AN INVITATION FROM ARENA MINA,
THE LIGHTHOUSE CAT

"The Lighthouse tower is open from 10:00 to 3:00.
Come see the Lighthouse, museum, gift shop, and me."

A True Story

It was during the end of August that Mina was discovered in the drainage culvert near the Assistant Keeper's Lighthouse lodging.

Someone had left the unwanted cat near the water tank. After three weeks, her new home was established at the Lighthouse, but she was missing a name.

The Lighthouse staff decided to hold an auction in order to name the cat. A long time benefactor and supporter, Pauline Zamboni, made the top ranking donation and chose the name, "Arena Mina." This name was selected in order to honor Pauline's granddaughter, Gelsomina, who lives in Lyon, France and is nicknamed, Mina.

The Point Arena Lighthouse

The Point Arena Lighthouse is surrounded by water on three sides. It is a very popular visitor destination in Mendocino County. It is located at 45500 Lighthouse Road in Point Arena, California, a beautiful coastal drive 130 miles north of San Francisco.

ENTRANCE

For my grandsons, Isaac, Ezra, Walter, and Bennett,
and for other boys and girls who like to rhyme.

Dedicated with many thanks to my loving husband,
Don, and to my illustrator, Adriane who gave me
support, encouragement, and the talent I needed to
complete this book. Also, to Brian Waters, my editor,
with gratitude.

Made in the USA
Middletown, DE
25 April 2021